YOUR KNOWLEDGE HAS VALUE

Alena Angelovicova

Trafficking in women

GRIN Verlag

Bibliografische Information der Deutschen Nationalbibliothek:

Die Deutsche Bibliothek verzeichnet diese Publikation in der Deutschen National-
bibliografie; detaillierte bibliografische Daten sind im Internet über http://dnb.d-
nb.de/ abrufbar.

Imprint:

Copyright © 2006 GRIN Verlag GmbH
Druck und Bindung: Books on Demand GmbH, Norderstedt Germany
ISBN: 978-3-638-78312-5

GRIN - Your knowledge has value

Der GRIN Verlag publiziert seit 1998 wissenschaftliche Arbeiten von Studenten, Hochschullehrern und anderen Akademikern als eBook und gedrucktes Buch. Die Verlagswebsite www.grin.com ist die ideale Plattform zur Veröffentlichung von Hausarbeiten, Abschlussarbeiten, wissenschaftlichen Aufsätzen, Dissertationen und Fachbüchern.

Visit us on the internet:

http://www.grin.com/

http://www.facebook.com/grincom

http://www.twitter.com/grin_com

Westminster University in London

Referat
Handout

Trafficking in women

by

Alena Angelovicova

2

The scope of the presentation on the trafficking in women

The main scope of the presentation is to outline the main theoretical perspectives of feminists on prostitution generally and prostitution in the context of sex-trafficking. I will consider some states to examine their legal provisions regulating prostitution (Israel, Sweden and the Netherlands) and I will focus on the international instruments covering trafficking in women. Then, the presentation will concentrate on the position of the UN office for drugs and crime in combating human trafficking and lastly it will examine the dichotomy of forced and voluntary prostitution in context with trafficking.

Theoretical and policy perspectives of feminists on prostitution generally and on the prostitution in context of trafficking in women

In generally, there are two feminist theories on prostitution itself and prostitution in the context of the trafficking in women; the structuralist perspective and the individualist perspective.

Structuralist perspective

(represented by radical approaches of Catherine McKinnon, Andrea Dworkin and Kathleen Barry) endorses the view of prostitution as modern-day-slavery and submission of woman to man. As stated by McKinnon (1993) "women are prostituted precisely in order to be degraded and subjected to cruel and brutal treatment without human limits"[1].(p.13) Thus, such a view necessarily considers prostitution as a form of trafficking in women where the consent of the woman as a "victim" to the prostitution is not important. In her book, Kathleen Barry carries out the view of the prostitution as form

---

[1] McKinnon, C., (1993). Prostitution and civil rights. *Michigan Journal of Law and Gender.* **1**, 13-32.

of slavery, well documented by the physical and psychological abuse and domination which fit to the definition of slavery.[2] The structuralist perspective (abolitionist approach) is represented by feminist organisation such as Coalition Against Trafficking in Women (hereinafter CATW) which denies the acceptance of prostitution as sex-work and prostitute as sex-worker with all rights applicable to her as to the employee. According to Janice Raymond of CATW, *"if women in prostitution are counted as workers, pimps as businessmen, and buyers as customers, then governments can abdicate responsibility for making decent and sustainable employment available to women."*[3] The important element of such concept is the responsibility of the state to support the education and to enhance the employment opportunities for women to ensure their worth and moral status. Structuralist approach thus not only suppresses the realisation of the individual self-determination of a woman and her choice to decide over her body but also further sets the state into the position of being the "social worker" responsible for a woman's well-being and her moral status.

Individualist perspective

(liberal approach) defends the possibility of consensual prostitution with legalization of sex-work by labor law, compulsory medical check-up, employment law and it strictly differs prostitution or sex-work from trafficking which necessarily involves element of coercion or force. The organisations representing such concept are the Global Alliance Against Trafficking in Women and Network of Sex Workers Project. The concept defends the right to self-determination, right to work, right to self-expression of the prostitute and the right of women to consent to commercial sex. It highlights the necessity to protect the labor and human rights of sex-workers by not putting them out of the scope of the provisions of law, but by regulating sex-work by law through ensuring some special rights evolving from the particular features of the sex-industry.[4]

---

[2] Barry, Catherine,(1979) *Female sexual slavery*.14

[3] http://www.brandeis.edu/projects/fse/Pages/traffickingdebate.html accessed on 21 of November 2006

[4] World Charter for Prostitutes Rights published by International Committee for Prostitutes Rights in Amsterdam in 1985 envisages rights and freedoms such as the right to protection against fraud, coercion and abuse, the right to proper working condition, the right to unemployment insurance, the right to self-

In the context with the trafficking it calls for the definition of trafficking in women covering the prostitution based on coercion or force.

The negatives and positives of abolitionism (structuralist approach) and individualism (legalization) towards prostitution and the trafficking in practice of Sweden, the Netherlands, and Israel

As pointed out by Hila Shamir in her study[5] of three countries in the context of their legal regulation of prostitution and trafficking, there are some positives and negatives of both, the abolitionism and individualism.

Sweden

The abolitionism, as presented in Sweden, considers it an offence to even just attempt to purchase sex. Swedish authoritative organs have declared the decrease of prostitution as a consequence of the strict regulation, but on the other hand the individualists have argued that prostitution went deeper underground, became unreported, worsened the working conditions, and greatened the dependence on pimps. Strict abolitionism in the eyes of the individualists takes very little responsibility for well-being of victims and while it protects some women, exposes others to the negatives of the illegal prostitution. According to the report of the UN office on drugs and crime in correlation with trafficking (2005), Sweden belongs to the group of countries where the incidence of reporting that country as the destination country of trafficking, occurs on the medium level.

---

employment, freedom to association, the freedom to travel, the right to the same tax regulation as other workers etc.; > http://walnet.org/csis/groups/icpr_charter.html accessed on 20-th of November 2006.
[5] Janet Halley, Prabha Kotiswaran, Hila Shamir, Chantal Thomas,(2006). From the international to the local in feminist legal responses to rape, prostitution/sex-work, and sex trafficking: four studies in contemporary governance feminism. *Harvard Journal of Law and Gender.* **29**, 336-419.

The Netherlands

In the Netherlands, the legalization of prostitution came into force in 2000 after the lifting of the ban on prostitution. However, the liberal approach towards prostitution doesn't cover the non-EU workers who remain thus the second class workers belonging to the illegal sector of prostitution. The Netherlands, however, is reported by the UN office of drugs and crime as a country with very high occurrence of the incidence of the destination country of trafficking.

Israel

Israel represents a hybrid of abolitionism and individualism and even without the legal regulation of prostitution; the regular sex-work remains non-prosecuted unless trafficking occurs. Abolitionism criticizes the state that it failed to protect women from violation of prostitution. Liberalism (individualists) criticizes the state for failing to protect sex-workers and their rights from negatives of illegal sex industry. The interesting fact of Israel, which just endorses the uncertainty of the quasi legalisation of the prostitution, is that despite the fact that Israel signed the 2001 Protocol to Prevent, Suppress and Punish Trafficking in Persons, Especially Women and Children, supplementing the United Nations Convention against Transnational Organised Crime it hasn't ratified it yet. Such a fact, thus, becomes very understandable in correlation with the report of the UN office on drugs and crime which reported Israel as a country with very high occurrence of the incidence of the destination country of trafficking.

International instruments on prostitution/trafficking in women

During the period of 1910-2003 were adopted several international instruments covering the scope of trafficking with particular impact on consent (distinguishing thus the voluntary prostitution from the forced one) as being part of the definition of trafficking. In generally, pre-UN Charter's international instruments on trafficking did not focus on consent in correlation with the regulation of trafficking.

6

1. In 1910 was adopted **International Convention for the Suppression of the White Slave Traffic which** criminalised trafficking with regard to only white race as being the victim.

2. 1949 **Convention for the Suppression of Traffic in Persons and of the Exploitation of the Prostitution of Others** doesn't consider the consent important for the determination of trafficking; the convention criminalizes trafficking regardless of the race of the victim, obligates states to take appropriate measures to prevent prostitution and to rehabilitate the victim; it consists of the provisions favorable to the structuralist approach (in the preamble of the Convention, it states the condemnation of trafficking for the purpose of prostitution as incompatible with the dignity and worth of the human person) and agrees to punish any person who "procures, entices or leads away, for purposes of prostitution, another person, even with the consent of that person and exploits prostitution of another person, even with the consent of that person."[6]

3. **The Convention on Elimination of All Forms of the Discrimination Against Women** (1979) in Art. 6 states neutral view of prostitution,[7] but Recommendation 19 of CEDAW supports the view of structuralist approach that consent is irrelevant, discourages commercial exploitation of women as sexual objects.[8]

4. 1993 **Declaration on the Elimination of Violence Against Women**, as first document to take a different than abolitionist approach, considers the violence of women inter alia trafficking in women and forced prostitution and takes a different approach from the UN Convention of 1949.

---

[6] Art. 1paras. 1, 2 The International Convention for the suppression of the traffic in persons and of the exploitation of the prostitution of others; UNGA Res. 317(IV) of 2-nd of December 1949 > http://www.ohchr.org/english/law/trafficpersons.htm accessed on 22-nd of November 1949
[7] In accordance with Art. 6 of CEDAW "States parties shall take all appropriate measures, including legislation to suppress all forms of traffic in women and exploitation of prostitution of women.
[8] Paras. 13, 14, 15, and 16 of the Recommendation 19 of CEDAW highlights the new form of sexual exploitation such as sex-tourism, organised marriages between women from developing countries and foreign nationals from developed countries and stress out that poverty and unemployment are the main factors force especially young girls to prostitution. It stresses out the vulnerability of the prostitutes to the violence, >http://www.un.org/womenwatch/daw/cedaw/recommendations/recomm.htm#recom19 accessed on 20-th of November 2006.

7

5. 2001 Protocol to Prevent, Suppress and Punish Trafficking in Persons, Especially Women and Children, supplementing the UN Convention Against Transnational Organized Crime adopts the definition of trafficking which broadens the concept of force and thus, the trafficking covers not only physical coercion but also the abuse of victim's position of vulnerability and not only sexual exploitation but also forced labour, slavery, servitude. The Protocol itself doesn't eliminate the concept of consent as a defence of prostitution. According to the Protocol, "Trafficking in persons shall mean the recruitment, transportation, transfer, harboring or receipt of persons, by means of the threat or use of force or other forms of coercion, of abduction, of fraud, of deception, of the abuse of power or of a position of vulnerability or of the giving or receiving of payments or benefits to achieve the consent of a person having control over another person, for the purpose of exploitation." Exploitation was given to include, at a minimum, forms of sexual exploitation, forced labor or services, slavery or practices similar to slavery, servitude or the removal of organs. The consent of a victim to the intended exploitation is irrelevant where any of the exploitative means have been used.[9]

It is interesting to point out the position of the Special Rapporteur on Violence Against Women who recognised the difference between the forced and the voluntary prostitution and as stated in report, "it is the non-consensual nature of trafficking that distinguishes it from other forms of migration".[10]

As we can conclude from the analysis of the international instruments regulating trafficking and as it is pointed out by Joe Dozeema

"there is no commitment in the UN to an integrated and coordinated prostitution policy and as a result, UN approaches are highly fragmented, with different UN instruments

---

[9] The Protocol to Prevent, Suppress and Punish Trafficking in Persons, Especially Women and children, supplementing the United Nations convention against Transnational Organised Crime adopted by UNGA Res. 55/25 from 15-th of 15-th of November 2000 which entered into the force in 2003 is signed by 117 states from which 110 the protocol ratified,
>http://www.unodc.org/unodc/en/crime_cicp_signatures_trafficking.html accessed on 20-th of November 2006.

[10] 2000 report of special rapporteur;
>http://www.ungchr.ch/Huridoca.nsflo/e29d45a105cd8143802568be005lfcfb/$FILE/60011334.pdf accessed on 23 of November 2006.

and bodies taking different ideological stances and even with contradictory positions within the same body or agreement."[11]

The position of the United Nations office on drugs and crime

The issue of trafficking, together with organised crime, has had significant impact on the world society and has become a global issue. The combat against human trafficking, as global problem, has been taken on board by the United Nations on international level.

The seriousness and global impact of human trafficking necessitated putting this problem on the agenda of the UN office for drugs and crime which adopted the Global programme against trafficking in human beings where it details the implementation of the Convention and 2001 Protocol (assessment of the national situation, legislative framework, human rights and anti-trafficking legislation, international criminal justice cooperation, non-criminalization of the victim of the trafficking, prevention of the trafficking through the awareness, the guidance for the states to adopt the measures in order to protect the victim of the trafficking such as housing, financial and legal aid). According to the 2005 Report of the UN office for drugs and crime, the category of very high incident of the origin countries of trafficking belongs to states of East Europe such Belarus, Bulgaria, Albania, Lithuania, Romania and Ukraine. In the category of the very high incident of states of destination of trafficking are the Netherland, Israel, Belgium, Germany, Greece, Japan, the USA, Thailand, Turkey, and Italy. Statistics show that in Thailand, Greece and the Netherland majority of the traffickers were nationals of these countries, which shows strong national connections to the destination country. Human trafficking for sexual exploitation is reported more frequently than human trafficking for forced labor.[12]

---

[11] Doezema. J. (1998), Forced to Choose Beyond the Voluntary v. Forced Prostitution Dichotomy. In Kempadoo Kamala and Jo Doezema *Global Sex Workers: rights, resistance and redefinition* (London: Routledge), pp. 36-47.

[12] www.unodc.org/unodc/en/trafficking_human_beings.html ,The United Nations office on drugs and crime (Toolkit to combat trafficking in persons, report Trafficking in human beings and the report on trafficking) The report of the UN office on drugs and crime is not comprehensive neither complex but its purpose is to stress out the importance for the data collection not from the international organisation but from states who seek to combat with the trafficking.

Indisputably, the great effort in combating the trafficking, especially in women and children, is produced apart from the UN, by the NGOs, such The Amnesty International or others NGOs which through projects or campaigns combat against the global issue of trafficking.

The dichotomy between the forced and the voluntary prostitution

The postmodern feminist theory (represented by Joe Dozeema or Yenwen Peng) refers to the negatives of the dichotomy of forced and voluntary prostitution in context with trafficking. The approach criticises the dichotomy of forced and voluntary prostitution which tends to widen the stigma of "whore" to which voluntary prostitute is generally referred to. The approach critises the organisations, promoting the self-determination of the sex-workers, of being highly focused on the elimination of forced prostitution in context with the trafficking and not on the rights of the sex-workers themselves. As pointed out by Yenwen Peng (2005)[13] *"sex-workers are disqualified from human rights consideration if their status is voluntary"* and such distinguishing can bear in extreme cases the threat of voluntary prostitutes being denied of their protection of human rights. The next negative element is the consideration of poverty as the force or coercion which makes the woman a helpless victim eligible for the protection of their human rights just because she "didn't choose" to be prostitute but she was forced by the indigence to do so. The dichotomy thus widens the difference between Western prostitute as being able to make a decision on being a prostitute and the third world woman the helpless, passive victim who is being "forced" into prostitution. But, in generally, slavery like conditions are problems also for those women who are already working in sex-industry and such dichotomy, when stretched to the maximum, can grant the protection of human rights to women on moral basis, favoring those who did not consent to being prostitutes and denying such protection to those who voluntarily choose to do so.

---

[13]Peng Y.,(2005),Of course they claim they were coerced: On voluntary prostitution, contingent consent and the modified whore stigma. *Journal of International Women's Studies,* **7**, 17-35.

Conclusion

Is the dichotomy of the forced and the voluntary prostitution substantive and beneficial to the regulation of trafficking? The first definition of trafficking as it is stated in 2001 Protocol appears to be a compromise between different views of structuralists and individualists. It recognises the voluntary prostitution indirectly, but stresses out also that such concept of consensus is irrelevant when one of the exploitative means (inter alia coercion, fraud, deception) is used. The regulation of trafficking thus cover the protection of those who are real victims of sexual exploitation, if it is woman who had consented to the prostitution and then became victim of sexual exploitation by working in slavery like conditions, or a woman who has been deceived and forced into sexual exploitation from the beginning. But, as it was pointed out previously in the criticism of the dichotomy of the forced and the voluntary prostitution, such dichotomy has its negative impact on the prostitutes as sex-workers. If the main purpose of the organisations supporting the self-determination of the prostitutes is to grant them the protection and status of sex-workers, then the more realistic approach will be to fight for such recognition on the international level through effective instruments of the International Labor Organisation[14].

---

[14] The ILO failed to recognised the sex-workers explicitly as workers but they recognised that where prostitutes are considered workers with rights under standard labor legislation, they are entitled to proper working conditions and to the protection from exploitation. In 1995 the ILO in its study, stated that the prostitution should be recognised as part of state's economy so it can be taxed.

Bibliography

1. Barry, K.(1979). *Female sexual slavery* in Halley J., Kotiswaran P., Shamir H., Thomas Ch.,(2006). From the international to the local in feminist legal responses to rape, prostitution/sex-work, and sex trafficking: four studies in contemporary governance feminism. *Harvard Journal of Law and Gender.***29**, 336-419.

2. Doezema, J., Forced to Choose Beyond the Voluntary v. Forced Prostitution Dichotomy in Kempadoo Kamala and Jo Doezema *Global Sex Workers: rights, resistance and redefinition* (London: Routledge, 1998), pp. 36-47

Articles

3. Balos B.,(2004). The wrong way to equality: Privileging consent in the trafficking of women for sexual exploitation. *Harvard Women's Law Journal.* **27**, 137-176.

4. Bindman Jo,(1997).Redefining Prostitution as Sex Work on the International Agenda (Anti-Slavery International). pp. 1-8, 27-29.

5. Cabezas, A.,(2000). Legal Challenges to and by Sex Workers/Prostitutes Symposium: Re-Orienting Law and Sexuality. *Cleveland State Law Review.* **48**, 79-92.

6.

   Cherry, A.,(2000). Welfare Reform and the Use of State Power in the Prostitution of Poor Women, Symposium: Re-Orienting Law and Sexuality. *Cleveland State Law Review.* **48**, 67-78.

7. Halley J., Kotiswaran P., Shamir H., Thomas Ch.,(2006). From the international to the local in feminist legal responses to rape, prostitution/sex-work, and sex trafficking: four studies in contemporary governance feminism. *Harvard Journal of Law and Gender.***29**, 336-419.

8. McKinnon, C., (1993). Prostitution and civil rights. *Michigan Journal of Law and Gender*. **1**, 13-32.

9. Peng Y.,(2005),Of course they claim they were coerced: On voluntary prostitution, contingent consent and the modified whore stigma. *Journal of International Women's Studies*, **7**, 17-35.

10. Zoglin K.,(1986) The UN action against slavery: A critical evaluation, *Human rights quarterly 8,* 306.

11. www.unodc.org/unodc/en/trafficking_human_beings.html ,The United Nations office on drugs and crime (Toolkit to combat trafficking in persons, report Trafficking in human beings)

12. The feminist sexual ethics project http://www.brandeis.edu/projects/fse/Pages/traffickingdebate.html